SEPTEMBER 2022

AN ANTHOLOGY OF ARTICLES

BRAIN BOOSTER ARTICLES

Contents

Preface

"Start writing, no matter what. The water does not flow until the faucet is turned on".

-Louis L'Amour

This book is a bouquet of articles contributed by students, professors and academicians. Hundreds of students and professors are contributing their work to Brain Booster Articles, we are here to provide ample information about Law and Contemporary issues. Our aim is to provide a platform for today's generation to express their views and ideas on law and contemporary law.

CHAPTER ONE

JUDICIAL ACTIVISM IN INDIA: ISSUES AND CHALLENGES

Author: Dr. Vivek Kumar, LLM,NET, LL.D, Deptt. Of Law DAV (PG) College Dehradun Uttarakhand

Co-author: Dr. J S Chandpuri LLM,NET,PhD, Deptt. Of Law DAV (PG) College Dehradun Uttarakhand

The judiciary is the cornerstone of the democracy which is an integral part of government. Judiciary is the third pillar of democracy but most important of the three organs of government. The constitution of India guarantees the fundamental rights and freedoms to all citizens, but these freedoms and rights have no significance unless there is a strong mechanism to enforce them, therefore judiciary plays a pivotal role to protect the human rights and their interests at the same time the judiciary keeps an eye on the activities of government. That's why the judiciary is also called vigilant sentinel of democracy. Public Interest Litigation (PIL) is the result of judicial activism. The judiciary has emphasized the importance of open government and rejected the privilege of government through judicial activism, the courts have also been restraints the government to misuse of their machinery. There are a number of cases, where judiciary has interfere the government affairs. Due to Judicial Activism, Article 21 of the constitution has become a Mini Constitution itself so far, consequently the ambit and dimension of article 21 of the constitution has become very elaborate. The role of judicial activism cannot be neglected or overlooked as it played a significant role in providing justice to the underprivileged sections of society, indigent individuals, socially and educationally backward classes, victims of trafficking and under trail prisoners, proper implementation of fundamental rights etc. could only become possible due to the advancement of judicial activism.

The Indian judiciary is playing a vital role of upholding citizen rights and implementing constitutional principles when the legislature and executive are fails to do so. Besides this judiciary has protest against the implementation of wrong policy and arbitrary laws of government. Due to its rational virtue and awareness, the judiciary has always raised its voice with majority against the encroachment of fundamental rights of citizens. On the other hand there is a narrow demarcation between activism and overreach, sometimes in the process of judicial activism the judiciary intervenes too much and reflects its personal belief in the course of providing justice. Due to judicial overreach, conflict takes place between the legislative, seems to be inactive or less competent to the people, the separation of powers on which the democracy stands is killed by the judicial overreach. Besides this there are so many socio-political issues which the judiciary is facing. Thousands of writs of Habeas Corpus as well as CAA, NRC cases and Article 370 are still pending, more than one lakh contempt cases as well as millions of pending cases has been lost their hope for the justice. It mostly said that the courts are working under the pressure of the governments. Cases in which the government itself is a party, are being here expeditiously, whereas matters related to the public are pending for many years. The present judiciary suffers from political interference. The law relating to UAPA and NSA are being misused openly and the judiciary remains silent in this regard. The judges are indirectly involved in political parties and are becoming the supporters of the government. However in a democracy, it is important to maintain the principle of separation of powers and uphold the three organs of government, at the same time the judiciary should be causes of stepping into spheres of activity that does not belong to it.

Conclusion

Thus, we can see that the higher judiciary is implementing the social interests with the highest priority. The role of judicial activism cannot be neglected or overlooked, it played a significant role in providing justice to the underprivileged sections of society, indigent individuals, socially and educationally backward classes, victims of trafficking and under trial prisoners, proper implementation of fundamental rights could only become possible due to the advancement of judicial activism. The Indian judiciary is playing a vital role of upholding citizens rights and implementing constitutional principles when the legislature and executive our fails to do so. Basically, the judiciary has protest against the implementation of wrong policy and arbitrary laws of the government due to its rational virtual and awareness, the judiciary has always raised its voice with majority, against such laws. But there is also a narrow demarcation between activism and overreach, sometimes in the process of judicial activism, the judiciary intervenes too much and reflects its personal belief in the course of providing justice. The interpretation of law start making the law, issues guidelines and directions which is to be done by the legislature.

Due to judicial overreach, conflict takes place between the legislature, seems to be inactive or less competent to the people. Besides this, the separation of powers on which the democracy stands is killed by the judicial overreach.1

Former supreme court justice, Mr. M. Katju is well known for his statements in society, although some people called his rhetoric, correct while many people also oppose it. Four judges of supreme court themselves had objected to the functioning of former chief justice of India Mr. Deepak Mishra. The impeachment motion against the former 4 judges of supreme court and High court was brought in parliament, although these resolution could never be passed by both the houses with majority, but points to a question mark on the independence of the judiciary. Former chief justice of Sikkim High court Mr. P. D. Dinakaran and Punjab & Haryana High court judge Nirmala Yadav are alleged misconduct of having acquired disproportionate assets. Dinakaran resigned from his post even before start of the impeachment.2 The impeachment motion was brought against the presiding judge of supreme court Mr. G. B. Pardiwala for his wrong remarks against schedule casts, when he was employed in Gujarat High court. Now he is in discussion with the harsh remarks in the Nupur Sharma hearing case, against, which many retired judges and many IAS themselves have a written letter to Supreme court.

In Kunal Kamara case, an interview was organised by DS4 'News exclusive channel' with an eminent advocate of supreme court Mr. Bhanu pratap singh, the brief description of this interview is being presented here, Mr. Bhanu Pratap Singh says, that the supreme court is not functioning fairly. In corona period, the words 'Satyamev Jayate' written on seal of the supreme court have been removed and 'Dharmo Dharme Rakshate' have been done. In the Ayodhya case, the supreme court itself accepted that even though there was no enough evidence in the favour of the temple, the verdict was executed in the favour of the temple by article 142, it simply means the protection of a particular religion under the leadership of the people of a particular religion. The issue of 8 justices was presented by Prashant Bhushan with evidence which was not heard but he was find rupee 1 for contempt of court. Cases, which in favour of government are heard immediately, while opposing cases are either dismissed or put on hold, they are never heard. Matter which is relating to Article 370 is pending for 4 years. Thousands of writs of habeas Corpus, CAA and NRC Cases are pending for a long time. The government are not implementing many cases decided by the various high courts and supreme court, more than 1 lakh contempt cases are pending in courts. Where, then the judicial activism of courts have been lost? The BJP has collected more than rupee 6000 crore through electoral bond and petition was filed regarding this but there is no hearing yet. Laws like UAPA, NSA are being misused a lot, INA puts whomever it wants in jail and leaves whomever it wants, no one to listen. Arnab Goswami was bailed out even in serious sections and many people like poets Barvara Rao, Sudha Bhardwaj, Anand Dev Tumse and Gautam Dev Naulakha are still in jail since many years for Bhima Koregaon case, they have been submitted application for bail before supreme court as many times, but still longing for bail.3 Barvara is 80 years old and urinates on the bed, he is a patient of Parkinson, supreme court has been rejected his bail, saying that approach the Bombay High court for bail. Barvara's only fault is that he works for the schedule tribe people of Jharkhand and which has been termed as maoist. Mr. Bhanu pratap singh has claimed that more than 2000 people are in jail without guilt for Delhi riots, not only this, there are 60 percent of people who are in jails of the country, for which there is no one to listen to them. Decisions are made only on cast and religious grounds. Attorney general K.K. Benugopal ji himself said in Prashant Bhushan case, that 5 judges accepted that the democracy is in danger and he personally knows 9 such judges with evidence, who are corrupt. At last, he pleads with folded hands to the judges that at least look at yourself with a cool mind, introspect and think that why the finger has started pointing at you. You cannot walk away from criticism. If your work impartially and fearlessly then of course you will not be criticized anywhere. The former Solicitor General of India Mr Deepankar P. Gupta, wrote (Hindustan Times June 15, 2007) that there is a real danger that the activism of the courts may aggravate the activism of the authorities. Today, inconvenient decision are left by the executive for the courts to take. Despite all these criticism, the judiciary has played an active role through its activism especially through PIL. This has restored the rights of disadvantaged sections of the society.

Hence it would to be appropriate to say that the scope of PIL is expending day by day against legislative and executive autocracy which indicates the spirit of judiciary. However in a democracy, it is important to maintain the principle of separation of powers and uphold the legitimacy of the three organs of government, at the same time, the judiciary should be cautious of stepping in to spheres of activity that does not belong to it.

1.https://www.legalserviceinindia.com

2. www.livehindustan.com 21. April2018, and aajtak.in

3. NDTV India 12 July 2022 : " The bail plea filed by P. Barvara Rao, has came up tohearing on 19 july, 2022 in this, the order of Bombey high court was challenged in which the court had refused to grant permanent medical bail"

CHAPTER TWO

ROLE OF FREEM AND FAIR ELECTIONS IN A DEMOCRACY

Author: Rohit Srivastava, III year of B.A.,LL.B. from Jamia Millia Islamia, New Delhi

INTRODUCTION

"The government of the people , by the people , for the people , shall not perish from the earth."

~Abraham Lincoln

In this article that is " role of free and fair elections in a democracy and its challenges", I have mentioned all the dimensions revolving around the topic. First of all I have done a brief discussion on what is democracy , how it is originated and how it is better than any other form of government and then I have discussed about the history of election and how the idea of election has reached world wide consensus. The given topic required exhaustive research and observation skills in order to give the appropriate conclusion at the end of the article.We can see the history of any country and can find how it has strived to get the form of government which is of the people , by the people and for the people. It is important to note the importance of election in a democracy and how the participation of people plays a significant role for making it successful. It is often said that democracy is not the best form of government but the better form of government compared to all the existing form of government that is monarchy, dictatorship etc. As there is fight to grasp power and share power in a democracy, times come when people tend to lead themselves in a corruptive way. As lord John Dalberg Acton has said, "power tends to corrupt, and absolute power corrupts absolutely", it is necessary to keep the eye on the exercise of power holding and power sharing through various mechanism like check and balance method in order to make most of the democracy.

WHAT IS DEMOCRACY ?

There is no exact meaning of democracy. The term expands its meaning according to place , time and circumstances. For general sense the word 'democracy' has been derived from two greek words that is "demos" which means people and kratos or cracy which means power or rule . Hence , the word democracy means rule by people. According to Cambridge dictionary , democracy is the belief in freedom and equality between people , or system of government based on this belief , in which power is either held by elected representative or directly by the people themselves.[1] Therefore , democracy is a form of government in which the real power is vested in the hands of people and power is exercised by them or by their elected representative under a free electoral system. At first, democracy originated in greek in the period of 5th century BC in the city of Athens. Later after travelling through seas it became prominent in other parts of the world. In earlier times, autocracy and oligarchies were only present in which power was kept in the hands of few who generally exploited the people and did not let other to take the hold of it. But in democracy there are generally large number of people contesting to come into power to do the functions of government. This often leads to the system of majoritarianisnm in which rule of people who are large in number began to suppress the demands of the one who are lesser in number. But most of the time, countries where constitution is there for the protection of rights the demands of minority are also taken into consideration. Meanwhile constitution acts as weapon or tool which takes the minority into account and guards there rights. Democracy is not only representation of people in a large number to give freedom of choice but also it is a form of government in which the aspects of liberty and equality are seen and protected. By establishing democracy a country can expect to form a government which could be stable for many years as the period of term of power specifies. This system of government ensures that the power is not kept in a hand of few for long period of time as lord Acton has said absolute power corrupts absolutely. In the preamble of the constitution of India there is a mentioning of "We the people..." which means that the sovereignty lies in the hand of people and people are responsible for the working of government. It is the people who are responsible to hold accountable the one who is not working properly in a democracy. There are many forms of democracy such as direct democracy, representative democracy , constitutional democracy and monitory democracy.[2] The history of a country decides the form of democracy which it choses. Many philosopher and thinkers have given their idea of democracy where their principles could be followed. An ideal democracy is the one in which rule of law prevails and there is an atmosphere of freedom of speech, freedom of movement, freedom to represent, right to elect and right to be elected in which each vote has equal value. Democracy as a form of government has a huge scope and it has various reason to be better than other forms of government. Now I would like to discuss further about the one of the most important component of democracy that is election.

<u>ELECTION</u>

The word election has come from a latin word "eligere" which means to pick out. In general sense election is a mechanism through which the members who stand to be elected in order to come into power are elected. Election are not used only for governmental purpose but for selecting leaders in various campanies and corporations. Elections acts as a major tool in forming the government in any modern democracy. In Vedic period of India, the Raja(chiefs) of a gana (a tribal organization) was apparaently elected by the gana. The Raja always belonged to the Kshatriya varna (warrior class) and was typically a son of the pervious Raja. However, the gana members had the final say in his election.[3] We can see that the idea of election is very archaic and it has come into lot of modification these days. Suffrage plays a very important role in every election. It is important to decide who gets to vote and what should be the value of it. In earlier times women were not allowed to vote in many countries but after waging a long battle, the right to vote was first given to women in the country of Netherlands. In 19th century the idea of universal adult suffrage surfaced according to which the right to vote is given to all citizens regardless of wealth, income, gender , social status, race , ethnicity, political stance or any other restriction subject only to relatively minor exception.[4] It is important to look at the trends and check whether the practice of election is taking place with the correct measures or not. Now I am going to discuss the importance of elections in a democracy and its challenges.

<u>IMPORTANCE OF ELECTION IN A DEMOCRACY AND ITS CHALLENGES</u>

Election plays the one of the most important system through which every democracy survives. It is way through which people gets the chance to chose their leader who will later form the government. In India election takes place in every five years. It gives the opportunity to people to select the one who they wish to be guided by. It gives people an opportunity to change its leader whenever the leader seems to go on corruptive way. Democracy is the form of government which is of the people , by the people and for the people and election forms the base through which the people get the chance to reflect themselves. Democracy without election is like a tiger without a tooth. It is no less better than autocracy or oligarchy in which power lies in the hand of few. No democracy can stand without free and fair election and there are large number of ways through which the election can get tampered. The one in power always wants to remain in power so for that he uses many viles and mean method to win the election. It is often seen that the rich candidates with criminal connections use any means to remove the other people who wants to stand in election. Moreover , it is mindset of the people which influence the way the one elects the people to form the government. People tend to ignore the good factors in the individual who can lead them on the path of development instead give the votes according to one's caste or creed. In recent times, cases have come in which the ways through which election took place that is through electronic voting machines seems to be hijacked. There is need to check the malpractices done in the election to make the democracy a powerful form of government.

CONCLUSION

Through the above discussion we can see that democracy is a best form of government among the other form of government. And election plays the one of the major role for the flourishing of democracy. It is important to take note of all the malpractices happening at the time of election so that free and fair election can take place. The election commission which is responsible for the conduction of the election should be sanctioned with more power. Moreover, a mechanism should be developed through which election commission does not get into the dirt of politics. At the end I would like to say that the people hold the most power in a democracy and it is the people who should always ask the question to the one who is in power so that proper balance of check and balance could be maintained and the ideals of democracy can grow.

Author's Biography

Hello! My name is Rohit Srivastava and I'am currently pursuing B.A.LLB.(hons.) course from Jamia Millia Islamia, Central University, New Delhi. My home town is Prayagraj which is famous for the amalgamation of three river which is Ganga ,Yamuna and Saraswati.

I am keenly interested in doing Social work and I am willing to work and fight for the rights of the under privileged. Moreover, I am devoted to the students who want to seek guidance for various entrance exam of prestigious Law Schools OF India. So, if incase somebody wants to come in contact with me in this regard he/she can mail me at the given email address at the end of this.

Email- rohitsrivastava341@gmail.com

CHAPTER THREE

REALITY OF THE REALTY SECTOR POST COVID -19 PANDEMIC

Author: Nirali Deepak Parekh, B.L.S ; L.L.B, Real Estate lawyer working with Damji Shamji Shah Group, Mumbai

When the country was enveloped by the Covid-19 pandemic, the Real Estate sector like many other sectors came to a complete standstill. With the central government imposing a nationwide lockdown, the builders were

forced to shut their project sites. Site visits were not permitted and construction activities too came to a total halt[i].The Indian Real Estate sector which was in the process of coming to terms with the various reforms brought by demonetization, GST, RERA etc. due to the lockdown it faced another major setback slowing down its growth momentum.[ii]

While it has been common for builders and developers to delay the projects and keep extending their timelines, due to the lockdown, it was inevitable that the ongoing projects would get further delayed. In order to aid the Real Estate sector during the lockdown, the central government and other regulatory bodies took steps to pacify the situation. Important notifications and guidelines were issued by different authorities including the MahaRERA from time to time and SEBI and the RBI also endeavored to provide some relief to the citizens during the upheaval.

The MahaRERA extended the validity period for registration of Real Estate projects, the completion dates or extended completion dates and also relaxed the time limits for statutory compliances from time to time to enable the developers /builders to cope up with the shutdown crisis[iii]. The alarming surge in the number of covid -19 cases made it difficult for the builders/ developers to adhere to the terms and conditions/ stipulations embodied / incorporated in the agreements entered into by them with the respective purchasers/ buyers etc. The Supreme Court of India acknowledged the Covid period as a 'Force Majeure'which gave a great relief to the developers/builderswho were paralyzed from fulfilling their obligations and/or promises and were unable to handover the possession to the flat purchasers on the date mentioned in their Agreements.The term 'force majeure' has been defined in the Black's Law Dictionary as 'an event or effect that can be neither anticipated nor controlled.' Some examples of force majeure events can be any kind of natural disasters like flood, earthquakes, quarantine, war etc.

The measures taken by various government authorities and other regulatory bodies providedsupport to the real estate market to sustain during the crisis. The Real Estate sector is largely dependent on various other industries to function. However, due to the mandated lockdown, the industries on which the Real Estate sector relies upon were not functioning. Thepandemic accompanied with the lockdown and restrictions on travel led to a disruption inthe supply chain of raw materials. The country also witnessed the plight of migrant workers returning back to their homes due to no source of income. The sector was already going through a major turbulence due to the subdued demand and liquidity crisis, policy reforms and structural changesbut the outbreak of the coronavirus followed by the mandatory lockdown, battered numerous industries all across the globe, including the real estate sector which was placed in dire straits.

Responsible central and state governments adopted various measures to lift up an economy witnessing a severe downfall. Real Estate sector was adversely hit by the imposition of the lockdown and its recovery waslargely dependent upon the steps which the government would take post the end of the pandemic for simmering the situation and regaining continuity in the business. The Indian Real Estate sector has been a significant contributor to the economic growth but however, the rampant spread of the coronavirus coupled with the mandated lockdown triggered an atmosphere of uncertainty, fear and panic leading to a delay in completion of projects and suspension of new launches. The threat of the contagion led to a stoppage of different businesses all across the globe, the real estate sector being no exception and was the most affected amongst all sectors. The investors kept a watchful eye, hoping that the customers would gear up towards a better future for reviving the Real Estate market,combating the catastrophe which had gripped the country.

The banks and various other financial institutions during the pandemic displayed reluctance to extend loans/financial aids to its customers as job security loomed over their customers which in turn compelled them to cancel the agreements entered into by them with the developers/builders. However, now as the economy has endeavored to restore a semblance of normalcy, the customers are regaining confidence with respect to job security and so we can conclude that the Real Estate sector in the post pandemic world is attaining stability to some extent and we are likely to see resurgence and reshaping of the industry in the near future.

Realty sector battles the economic slump emerged due to Covid -19 and navigates its way to stabilize in the market by taking necessary steps and measures pivotal for its survival and sustainability once again!!

[i]https://sciendo.com/pdf/10.2478/bjreecm-2021-0010 Article by Rashmi JayminSanchaniya. [ii]https://api.anarock.com/uploads/research/ANAROCK_Covid-19%20Impact%20on%20Indian%20RE%20Sector.pdf [iii]https://www.business-standard.com/article/pti-stories/covid-19-maharera-extends-completion-deadline-for-real-estate-projects-by-3-months-120040201392_1.html

<u>Author's Biography</u>

My name is Nirali Deepak Parekh. I am a Real Estate lawyer working with Damji Shamji Shah Group, Mumbai (in house legal department). I have been writing legal articles since the year 2017 for 'The Legal Services India'. I have also given my work for various national as well as an international law journal and achieved many awards too by the Legal Services India.

CHAPTER FOUR

CONCEPTUAL ANALYSIS ON CONCURRENT EXPERT WITNESSES IN INTERNATIONAL ARBITRATION

Author: Khuloos Aziz Chawla, pursuing LL.M. in ADR from Jindal Global Law School, O.P. Jindal Global University, Sonepat

The method of Concurrent Expert Witness or Hot-Tubbing originated in Australia and was initially practiced in Australian Competition Tribunal. From its application in Australian Trade Practices to officially being introduced in Federal Courts of Australia it became one of the most important rules throughout the world. This concept seeking much attention in the various court systems, is now also gaining a room in Alternative Dispute Mechanism.

Hot-Tubbing is a process of gaining the expert advice and the experts are sworn to give the competent opinion within their expertise capacity so that the same can be relied upon without any delay. It can also be called as "Concurrent Expert Witness" Tandem Expert" and "Dueling Experts"; these individuals that are stated as experts must be of the competent capacity in their respective field.It is a method where experts give their advice, and the arbitrator discusses it. When the written statements along with evidence are done then only experts are called upon to give their statements regarding the concerned issue. The experts can be called from both the sides, they present their facts and figures, and later arbitrator or leading counsels may ask questions relating to the subject matter. Also, the judge can ask questions in between but the rules of examining the expert witness may differ from each country.

How it is Different from Traditional Method of Evidencing?

Hot-Tubbing method in arbitration is very different from the traditional method of evidencing in litigation. The experts are made to testify from both proposing and opposing sides, they are brought together and are supposed to prepare their side of written reports. These reports are then exchanged, and they are directed to make joint statements together. This process eliminates the grounds of disagreement between the two and only present the summary of issues on which both the experts agree. Before the trial starts, both the parties produce an agreed agenda for taking concurrent evidence based on the joint statement. When the hearings start at the trial court, experts are sworn and placed in front of each other at the witness table. The issues on which there is a disagreement between the experts, those questions are directed to the arbitrator beforehand. The experts are encouraged to answer the questions addressed by their expert on the opposite side and the counsels. The cross-examination, re-examination or clarifying sessions can be done from these experts' witnesses. However, the counsels' participation is only restricted to raising objections and no questions on any other or new issues shall be asked.

Hot-Tubbing: Double-Edged Sword

Hot-Tubbing of experts is a double-edged sword as it has its own pros and cons. This process is rapidly growing in the field of arbitration as this method is more in tune of a dialogue rather than a verbal battle between the witness and the counsels. Arbitration itself is a speedy process and having expert's opinion makes it easier for the tribunal to reach to the roots of the cause more constructively by investing less time and efforts. The tribunal dons the hat of the leader of the discussion as it supports impartiality, eliminates biasness, increases responsiveness and it is precise to only knowledgeable area by expert advice. Furthermore, the involvement of such competent persons ensures better assessment of the matter and highlights the discrete issues that needs coherence. On the other hand, the downside of Hot-Tubbing includes that it should only have the fully prepared experts, they should possess full knowledge of the subject matter and have skepticalanalyzing skills otherwise the whole meaning of expert advice will go in vain. Experts should be well trained with the court etiquettes to maintain the decorum of the court room as their demeanor plays a pivotal role and if it isn't adhered to, then proceedings will not serve the true purpose. Experts ought to be formal and respective towards the arbitrator. Lastly, Hot-Tubbing makes the process of arbitration more costly as experts that are engaged also have their charges that are added and due to lack of formal examination during the whole process, the arbitrator might miss the key evidence.

<u>International Recognition</u>

Hot-Tubbing of experts is internationally gaining popularity and many arbitration tribunals worldwide have laid down their own rules for smooth application and promoting the expert advice. However, it is not mandatory under the process of any International Arbitration institution but a preferred act as it enhances the clear approach in the matter.

Hot-Tubbing has gained the legislative meaning as International Bar Association (IBA) in its Rules of Evidence in International Arbitration 20201recognizes the terms such as "Expert Report", "Party-Appointed Expert" and "Tribunal Appointed Expert". Also, Article 5(3A) of IBAstates that "the Arbitral Tribunal in its discretion may order that any Party-Appointed Experts who have submitted Expert Reports on the same or related issues meet and confer on such issues. The Article 8(4)(f) of IBA has directly mentioned the Hot-Tubbing by stating that "the Arbitral Tribunal, upon request of a Party or on its own motion, may vary this order of proceeding, including the arrangement of testimony by particular issues or in such a manner that witnesses be questioned at the same time and in confrontation with each other (witness conferencing)".The rules also provide the various methods for the testimony of the experts at the evidence stage.

Chartered Institute of Arbitrators (CIArb) has published the Guidelines for Witness Conferencing in International Arbitration2. The rules aim to provide a non-exhaustive checklist of the factors that are to be considered in establishing a procedure that will govern the efficient and effective taking of evidence from experts. These are basically the procedural orders that can be used as the criteria for appropriate administrative directions for witness conferencing.

Apart from Australia where this practice was originated, the Canadian Evidence Act3 and Canadian International Trade Tribunal4 (CTT) Rules recognise the concept of expert witness. The CTT Rules give the discretion to the tribunal to testify the experts and promote the open discussion and question relating to the facts in issue. There are proper rules laid down to establish the method of Hot-Tubbing of expert witnesses.

Indian Perspective

The concept of Hot-Tubbing is a well-known method in Indian. The Section 45 of Indian Evidence Act 18725 acknowledges the expert's opinion. The law stipulates the grounds as to when the experts can be referred for the advice, such as the issues relating to science, handwriting, foreign law, art or any other. Accordingly, experts shall be the skilled personnel whose opinion are valued but are not conclusive. Similarly, the opinion as well as the expert itself can be cross-examined.

Hot-Tubbing is also permitted in the commercial dispute as according to the amended Delhi High Court (Original Side) Rules, 20186, Section 6 under Chapter XI. These rules empower the court on its own or by the application of parties to permit the testimony of experts by the way of witnesses. The mechanism to regulate the process is mentioned under Annexure G of the rules and court may in its discretion mould the process according to the need of the dispute.

The landmark case in which Hot-Tubbing was addressed by the Delhi High Court was Micromax Informatics Limited vs Telefonaktiebolget L M Ericsson7. In this case courtemphasized on nature and scope of Hot-Tubbing as the dispute was related to Patent Law wherein parties had the wish to adopt the method of Hot-Tubbing. The court stated that "With respect to the procedure that can be used to arrive at a swifter resolution of disputes (such as in patent cases, involving technology and scientific experts" testimony and evidence), this court is of the opinion that patent disputes and those that involve examination of expert evidence should adopt the hot-tubbing procedure."

Conclusion

Hot-Tubbing is the process that is still emerging and is in the middle of the road to the way of development in International Arbitration. There is an immediate need to make the procedures more stringent to take experts advice 'mandatory' in the matters needing professional opinion. The International Arbitration Institutions should adopt rules relating to application of the expert advice if it is the requirement of the case. Being a growing scenario, it will surely create an ease for the courts and tribunals.

With the rapid growth of this concept in India, Arbitration and Conciliation Act 1996 needs to have the concrete provision relating to Hot-Tubbing. However,Section 19 of Arbitration and Conciliation Act

19968mentions that the tribunal is not bound by the procedural or evidentiary law of the country and the parties are free to agree on the procedure to be followed by the arbitral tribunal. This section indirectly creates the advantage of taking the expert advice in any of the given scenario. In the nutshell, India is making its way in adapting the concept of Hot-Tubbing as it is evident from the rules of the Delhi High Court, but Indian legal regime needs more restrictive paradigm shift to make it a combative model in future for the world.

<u>Author's Biography</u>

Khuloos is currently pursuing LLM in Dispute Resolution from Jindal Global Law School, which is one of the elite law schools in India. She has a keen interest in Arbitration, Litigation, and International Commercial Arbitration. Prior to joining JGLS, Khuloos was working as a legal intern in Dua Associates and at various other Law offices. She has completed her B. Com LLB (Hons.) from Amity Law School Noida, where she was one of the Batch Toppers. She was the President of the Alternative Dispute Resolution society at Amity Law School Noida. She had actively contributed to society, by heading National Tournaments and representing herself in various National Competitions, and winning a few. Apart from this, she has been throughout scholarship student and has won several debate competitions.

Khuloos is a member of various National and International Arbitration organizations. She has been training school kids and adjudicating the debating rounds for them. She has also written a lot of Research papers, articles, and blogs. One remarkable achievement of her includes being awarded the Gold Medal for the Best Research Paper on the sensitive issue of Triple Talaq. Her interest areas include Alternative Dispute Mechanisms, Human Rights Law, and Commercial Disputes

CHAPTER FIVE

SOCIO-LEGAL ISSUE IN INDIA

Author: Radhika Dwivedi, II year of B.B.A.,LL.B.(Hons.) from NMIMS, Indore

India is a country of diversities. Different religions, castes, traditions, languages, cultures and entangled social fabric are visible in India. The slavery of foreigners for centuries has produced many evils in Indian society. In particular, issues like casteism, women's protection, communalism, economic inequality, religious bigotry and poverty, hunger remain the social legal issues of our great country.

Legal empowerment and justice system a historical phenomenon and has developed basis societal conditions and changes from time to time over centuries. Social justice is hence a critical factor in the legal justice system and its coverage. As the society matures, more and more social issues are taken care by Judicial System and tries to solve them. Few of the issues are being discussed here under.

1. RACISM

The Constitution of India gives equal rights to all citizens at social, economic, political and education levels. All citizens have equal rights. At any level, there can be no discrimination against any citizen. But in reality, the country is still far away from this legal right. Even after seventy years of independence, there is discrimination among citizens at some legal level, at some social level. The caste system in India has its roots in ancient India. In ancient India, rules and duties in terms of a person's life, varna or caste were determined by his actions. All professions were the same. Everyone was seen with respect, but first the faulty system of the Mughals and later the British divided the society into permanent castes. Today is the biggest social legal challenge of the country. The society is divided into upper and lower castes.

Discrimination is highly tragic for the lower castes. Socially it is abusive. At the same time, reservation has been provided to the following castes in the name of social equality. It reduces the right of upper-class people. This is a big issue. If the upper class is demanding the abolition of reservation, then the lower class wants more rights over resources by giving their discriminatory past. Even after seven decades of independence, there has been no consensus in the country on this issue. According to me this is India's biggest social legal issue.

2. INEQUALITY

The constitution gives equal right to both men and women in every field. Women have been given many rights after independence. [1]Right to vote, right to legal marriage, inheritance of property, divorce, dowry rights. The Equal Remuneration Act was passed in 1976 to provide equal remuneration to men. Muslim women have recently gained rights against triple talaq. But even after getting the legal strength at social level, women are facing many challenges socially.

The right to equal labor is only on paper. In the private sector, women are generally less working than men. The situation is that even if a seat is secured in an election in rural areas and she wins and holds a position, her husband or relatives takes the responsibility in her place. Although these Kurutis are slowly decreasing but at a very low slow pace. Women have the right to equal share in property. But 80 per cent of the women in the country still do not get a share in the property of the mother and father. In rural areas, this percentage is more than 95 per cent. If a woman asks for her share, only relatives oppose her. Women are now getting more opportunities than ever before in sectors like military and defense. But this opportunity is available only to limited area and limited women. In rural areas, women are still struggling for education and equal opportunities.

3. ECONOMIC DISPARITY

Economic disparity is a challenging social legal issue in India. According to the Global Wealth Report, 10 per cent of India's rich people own 77.4 percent of the country's wealth. On the other hand, 60 per cent of the people own only 4.7 per cent property. 6 percent of these people are those whose income is less than hundred rupees. [2]Millions of people still do not have the bread for two days. At the same time only ten percent people have acquired two-thirds of the country's wealth. This inequality destroys the fabric of the country. Increases poverty and unemployment. Social harmony also ends because of this inequality. As such, everyone has the right to live legally and live honorably. But at the ground level it has many punchdiggies. It does not look the same on the ground.

4. RURAL AND URBAN DIVIDE

The country's major social challenge is that 70 percent of the population in India lives in the village. But in the name of facilities, there is not even thirty percent facilities as compared to cities. The agricultural sector is continuously backward and youth are migrating continuously to the cities. Farming has become a continuous loss. There are several thousand villages in the country where only the elderly is left to live. The youth have left the villages in the hope of employment and better facilities. The reason for this is the lack of facilities in rural areas. The youth who lead a livelihood by farming are troubled. Because of this, the farmers want to get more facilities and discounts through constant agitation. In recent days, farmers are agitating all over the country on the issue of support price and free market.Discrimination in urban and rural life remains a big challenge and social issue before the country.

5. RELIGIOUS FUNDAMENTALISM

Originally, India is a country of people living in harmony, harmony and equality with all religions and all castes. But for some decades religious fundamentalism has challenged the integrity and unity of the country. The incidents of maw leaching along with religious riots and terrorist incidents have spoiled India's name in the world. Legally, governments are dealing with convicts influenced by fundamentalist ideology, yet religious segregation in all the states of the country poses a major challenge. Similarly, caste-sharing is also a big issue. For example, when the Supreme Court made changes in Section 3 a few years ago, there was uproar in the whole country. Police have the right to arrest anyone without investigation on the report of Scheduled Caste Scheduled Tribes. It was the subject of arrest only after being investigated. But the change was not liked and there were fierce movements across the country. There are many issues which still remain social legal issues before the country. Apart from this, many social legal issues have been emerging in India. Issues like workers' rights, children's rights, dowry system, unemployment, illiteracy, starvation, remain a challenge even after centuries

6. LINGUISTIC DIVERSITY

As I said, India is a country full of diversities. There are around 121 major languages, spoken by groups[3]. Apart from the languages included in the Eighth Schedule of the Constitution, each state has its own mother tongue. There are 60 languages whose number of speakers is more than one million. This is also the beauty of the country, as well as trouble for the unity of the country. The mother tongue of India is Hindi. But there is strong opposition to Hindi in South Indian states. The protest is of such a level that if the names of railway stations, banks or public places are written in Hindi then there will be uproar. North Indian citizens do not feel familiar in South India and South Indian citizens in North India. The same is with the residents of the Indian states of the North East.

Recently, when the central government formulated an education policy, it was recommended to include Hindi in primary education. There was a sharp reaction in the South Indian states. The Center had to clarify that this was not mandatory. This attitude is towards Maharashtra's Marathi, West Bengal's Bengali, Odisha's Oriya. There is also linguistic radicalism in Tamil, Malayalam, Telugu, Assamese linguistic states. Because of this, India could never be integrated into linguistic unity.

7. NAXALISM

I am from Chhattisgarh. The major challenge of Chhattisgarh is Naxalism flourishing here. Naxalism is deeply affected in Madhya Pradesh, Maharashtra, Odisha, Jharkhand and Andhra Pradesh adjoining Chhattisgarh and Chhattisgarh. Till now thousands of people have lost their lives in Naxal attacks. It is a socio-economic and legal dispute. Naxalites do not believe in the Constitution of India even while living in the country. They demand that full rights of water, forest and land should be given to the people living there. Make decisions there. They should have power there. The tribals in particular should be empowered to govern and control the natural resources. It is against the Constitution of India. Because of this, the Government of India has deployed about 50 thousand paramilitary forces in Chhattisgarh itself. Apart from this, more than 30 thousand soldiers are deployed in border states.

Tribals lose their lives in a war between jawans and Naxalites. The martyrdom of hundreds of soldiers has been done so far and the Naxalites have also lost their lives. All of these people are citizens of India who die. But this tension has not ended because of disagreements with the law. This social legal issue remains a major obstacle in India's development.

8. SEPARITISM AND TERRORISM

Similarly, terrorist attack in Kashmir is also a social legal issue. A group of citizens there challenge the power of India. He keeps demanding the independence of his kingdom. However, because of the abolition of Article 370 recently, terrorism in Kashmir has reduced considerably. But it is yet to be fully controlled. In many states of the Northeast, small groups clash with governments because of hostility. Their demands are local. And socially they keep demanding complete independence. Organizations like United Liberation Front of Assam, National Democrat Front of Bodoland in Assam keep demanding separate statehood. In many states like Manipur, Tripura, Nagaland, extremist organizations are active about their demands. These organizations see their existence as a separate country on linguistic, cultural and geographical basis. However, the central government has always kept open the way for limited power usage and dialogue with these organizations. Because of this, many extremist organizations have formed a mindset to fulfill their demands while staying in India. But these still remain stressful social legal issues for the country.

CONCLUDING REMARKS

Social issuesare a problem that influences the common citizen of a country and as Justice is a fundamental pillar of Indian Democracy and Constitution, the law makers and law keepers need to be proactive to cater to the social injustice and inequalities from time to time

Social issue can be a part of our history, traditions and cultural stereotypes. And every country in the world faces different social issues like racism, illiteracy, inequality etc. so is India. India being an old civilization with multiple rulers from time to time, has its own social issues. Unfortunately, in the modern world more than 29% of Indians live in poverty. Hence it is utmost duty of all citizen the true civilizational values of Social Justice

Lastly, Social issue, if they are not solved can lead to dissatisfactions, disruptions and violence.As we all move towards a new millennial with technology as a new normal, social legal issues will take newer forms and shapes. We have to prepared to tackle the same as always.

[1]IMPORTANT CONSTITUTIONAL AND LEGAL PROVISIONS FOR . Retrieved September 29, 2021, from http://mospi.nic.in/sites/default/ files/reports_and_publication/cso_social_statices_division/ Constitutional&Legal_Rights.pdf [2]Richest 10% of Indians own over 3/ 4th of wealth in India. Retrieved September 29, 2021, from https://www.livemint.com/Money/iH2aBEUDpG06hM78diSSEJ/ Richest-10-of-Indians-own-over-34th-of-wealth-in-India.html [3]More than 19,500 mother tongues spoken in India: Census | India . Retrieved October

1,   2021,   from   https://indianexpress.com/article/india/more-than-19500-mother-tongues-spoken-in-india-census-5241056/

ENVIRONMENTAL CRIME AND THE LAW; HOW THESE LAWS CAN BE STRENGTHENED TO ACHIEVE SUSTAINABILITY?

Author: Heeral Devpura, IV year of B.B.A.,LL.B.(Hons.) from Amity University Rajasthan

Abstract

Environmental crime is the violation of laws designed to protect the environment and human health. These laws regulate air and water quality and dictate how the disposal of waste and hazardous materials can be done legally. Sustainable development creates a framework in which people can live and thrive in harmony with nature, rather than living at the expense of nature, as we have done for centuries. However, despite the many existing environmental and natural resource laws, sustainability does not have an adequate or supportive legal basis today. If we want to make significant progress on the way to a sustainable society, let alone achieve sustainability, we have to develop and enforce laws and legal institutions that do not exist today or that exist in a completely different form. In order to achieve sustainability, we must also recognize that environmental law, while key to achieving sustainability, is only a part of necessary legal framework. Other legal foundations pertain to a wide range of other laws, including land tenure and use laws, tax laws, laws affecting our government structure, and the like. This issue of sustainability is not just about the relationship between law and sustainability. The patrons to this issue also try to answer the question of how the law can and should be used to achieve sustainability in different ways. Basically, the "Law for Sustainability " is also about governance for sustainability, because the law provides essential instruments and institutions to govern sustainably.

Keywords: environmental law, sustainability, sustainable development, law for sustainability, law, legal institution, environmental crimes

Introduction

Environmental crime is widely recognized as one of the most profitable forms of transnational crime. Environmental crime is increasing and efforts to prevent it should increase as well. Functional criminal law also aims to deter and generally prevent such activities. There are several reasons why existing laws have not been effective in curbing environmental crime. There are a variety of problems faced by those tasked with enforcing these laws. There are several loopholes in the dual role of agencies, which are both advisers and enforcers of these laws. In addition, there are problems that prosecutors and police face when investigating the jurisdiction and responsibility of the accused. These concerns seek clarity about the underlying causes of these fundamental issues. Therefore, this article examines whether criminal law can help protect our environment by acting as a means of monitoring and controlling dangerous activities that directly or indirectly affect the environment. It focuses on how effective the regulatory aspects of the law are, the likelihood of sanctions and penalties, and their severity in actually deterring such activity.

Introduction to Environmental laws

These laws deal with the regulatory web, the general principles that govern them, and the customary laws that describe the impact of human activities on the environment. These laws mainly work on the idea of pollution as the centre of all implementation. They recognize our natural resources, their scarcity, the need to conserve them for future generations and generally work for environmental impact assessment.

For India, our environmental laws mainly focus on areas related to air pollution and quality, water pollution and quality, sustainable development, waste management, preventive and preventive measures, elimination of pollutants, safety in discharge and treatment of discharge of chemical elements and public Trust. However, its implementation involves much more complex problems, where social, political and economic factors combine to address serious environmental impacts. All of these environmental rights and principles have been behind the development of environmental jurisprudence and judicial jurisprudence in the country. This existing framework is used to mediate the role of the various public and private companies and to determine their constitutional, statutory and customary application and performance.

In the context of the country's efforts to respond to increasing environmental degradation, there is a conceptual clarity about the laws, the gaps, their application, the obstacles and limitations they face that are relevant to improving the environment, required quality of the environment. the country's environmental policy.

<u>**Environmental Crimes**</u>

Environmental crime encompasses a wide range of offenses that harm the environment and human life, from administrative or recordkeeping errors to the actual dumping of pollutants into the environment illegally. Environmental crime may include, but is not limited to[1] the following:

i. Poaching

ii. Unreported fishing

iii. Unlawful trade in wildlife

iv. Trade in unregulated and illegal products for financial and personal gain: trade in timber, ivory, rhino horn or even sandalwood

v. Oil spills

vi. Littering

vii. Destruction of wetlands

viii. Dumping into oceans, streams, lakes, or rivers

ix. Irregular waste disposal

x. Inappropriately handling pesticides or other toxic chemicals

xi. Unethical removing and disposing of asbestos

xii. Falsifying lab data pertaining to environmental regulations

xiii. Burning garbage

xiv. Confiscating certain chemicals, such as CFC refrigerants, into the U.S.

xv. Committing fraud related to environmental crime

So far, the environment has been heavily impacted by human activities, the damage caused is irreparable, but it can still be repaired if people understand the following statistics

- Every year, people consume more than 50 billion tons of natural resources
- At the rate of deforestation, increasing whatever the purpose, the rainforest will only be around for the next 80 years, after that we won't have a rainforest anymore, they are responsible for a large percentage of the fresh oxygen we humans live on.
- In 2020, people eliminated almost 10 million tons of hazardous waste.
- According to some predictions humans will need another planet like earth to support life on the real earth, we are consuming the near future, we are consuming the entire planet. But people don't realize that they only have one.
- Humans have consumed more than half of coral reefs and are consuming at a rising rate. There will be no more coral reefs in the next 30 years. They are being lost due to human activities causing seawater temperature rise, acidification and algae.
- By 2050, humans will lose all of their fisheries, which are the lungs of the planet.
- Humans eat, destroy and consume more than 2 billion innocent animals and plants every week.
- Humans are responsible for killing more than ten thousand species of animals and plants every year.
- Almost 50,000 litres of fresh water are needed to produce 1 kg of meat.

Legal framework

The crime against the environment implies the violation and disobedience of pre-existing laws and laws aimed at protecting the ecological balance of nature. The pursuit of the rich, ever richer and richer, in the name of development and society's ever-increasing capitalist idealism has conveniently managed to reach this troubling state of dangerous profligacy. There are a variety of laws introduced by the legislature and government to protect the environment.

To name a few, these include the Water (Pollution Prevention and Control) Act[2], the Environment (Protection) Act[3] (enacted after the Bhopal gas tragedy), the Water (Prevention and Pollution Control) act[4], the (Pollution Prevention and Control) Act[5] etc. Despite this broad legal landscape with a wide spectrum of legislation, there are countless loopholes and loopholes in the shocking application of these sanctions and penalties to environmental crimes. For example, India is a signatory member of five major international wildlife conservation conventions, but there are many instances where illegal trade in endangered animals has taken place between neighbouring countries. All of this targets one thing: institutional failure and legislative inadequacy, and hence, despite so many enforcement provisions, the criminal sanction has proven ineffective.

Constitution and judicial intervention

Under the title "Fundamental Duties and Guiding Principle of State Policy" (DPSP), India is working on its national obligation to promote environmental protection. These articles were a guide for the country to ensure a healthy environment for its people. All these edicts, laws and their application are the result of many litigations of public interest based on the principle settled by court under Article 21 of the Indian Constitution, which recognizes the fundamental substantive right to a healthy and pollution-free environment[6].

Furthermore, it was the 42nd Amendment that introduced the word Environment into the Indian Constitution along with Article 48A of the DPSP and Article 51A among the Basic Duties[7].

Article 48A- It is in Part IV of the Constitution of India, under the guiding principles of state policy, it is entitled Protection and Improvement of the Environment and Protection of Forests and Wildlife. It is interoperable that the government has a responsibility to protect the forest and wildlife. The court has the power to impose economic sanctions on wrongdoers, but recently they have started using incarceration as a tool under the jurisdiction of the court and the intensity of the crime.

Article 51A- under Part V of the Indian Constitution, under the basic duties, it is referred to as the basic duties, a duty (g) has been added, which is interpreted as meaning that people have a duty and obligation to the environment, viz They must protect rivers and wildlife and have compassion for all living beings around them.

Criminal Remedies: The following are the Criminal Remedies under the Indian Penal Code The following sections of the IPC, 1860 deal with public safety, public health, public nuisance, negligence:

• Section 268 to-Section 294-A

• Section 269-271- spread of infectious disease is a public nuisance and a crime

• Section 277- preventing water pollution

• Section 290- Smoking in public is a crime

• Section 426-Pollution caused by mischief

- Section 430-Pollution caused by mischief
- Section 431-Pollution caused by mischief
- Section 432-Pollution caused by mischief

All of these are crimes and these crimes are public in nature, meaning they are against the state. The remedies used are economic sanctions, imprisonment, or both

Significant Amendments in Environmental Law in India

There have been some major, important and recent changes in the National Environmental Law of India, these changes are as follows. These laws have both relaxed and imposed restrictions.

- As part of the Environmental Impact Assessment in 2006, it helped loosen infrastructure, but at the expense of massive dangers, before this change almost all large projects were required, but now the projects covering the area less than 50,000 square meters are not. require prior official approval.
- An amendment was introduced in the Coastal Ordinance[8] which helped increase tourism in India, but again at the expense of the environment. In this government, the requirement for prior government approval for starting such a project in the coastal regions has been removed. The above laws eased government restrictions. Listed below are the changes that have helped the government to enact proper regulations in environmental policy. They are as follows:
- The Motor Vehicles (Amendment) Act[9] - This Act focuses specifically on increasing the penalty for violators of all motor vehicle laws, z 100 in front of the people who were required to knock Rs.100 now had to pay Rs. 1000 for the same crime, this law had a great impact, people began to obey road laws and proper equipment in cars to avoid environmental damage. But various states in India came full circle when they changed state laws in, returning fines for political and social benefits to nominal rates.
- Factories Act 1987 - this was a much-needed law that brought strict laws on factories mainly responsible for environmental degradation after the Bhopal gas tragedy, and strict steps were taken in the drafting of these laws to ensure adequate control over the factories maintain factories to see whether the basic standards are met or not.

Case Laws

1. Municipal Council, Ratlam v. Vardhichand and Others[10]Also known as the Ratlam City case, considered a landmark and very important ruling by the Supreme Court of India, in this case the court dealt with the effect of the deteriorating urban environment on the poor living in the area public health recognized as a human right, which forced the local council to take appropriate action, particularly in the management of the drainage works in Ratlam.

2. M.C Mehta v. Union of India (Shriram Industries Case)[11]Also referred to as the Shriram gas leak case. This was thecase of gas leak of edible chemicals in the capital of the country, New Delhi. During this case the court ascertained that company in below absolute liability, to pay the compensation to the victims of the gas leak, this was the primary case in India, within which the thought of absolute liability was introduced. This was conjointly the first case in India in which the defendant was penalized, and was asked to obtain the injury caused, and pay compensation to the victims of the gas leak.

3. M.C Mehta v. Union of India (Ganga case)[12]Also referred to as the Ganga pollution case, this is often a case, that is taken into account to be the foremost important case, for rivers associate degreed their rights. During this case the court ascertained, and closed several tanneries around and within the town of Kanpur, Uttar Pradesh, as Ganga is one among the biggest rivers in India, there are many industries, which cause pollution. Justice E.S. Venkataramiah observed rather like a business which cannot pay minimum wages to its staff cannot be allowed to exist, a workplace which cannot setup a primary treatment plant cannot be permissible to still be in existence.

4. Tarun Bharat Singh, Alwar v. Union of India and Others[13]In this case, the court banned mining in the region of Sariska National Park, but unfortunately, according to reports from 2015, mining in Sariska is in full swing and causing environmental damage. And no appeal has been lodged with the Supreme Court, not even against Article 21, which guarantees the right to a safe and healthy environment.

<u>Principles Guiding Environmental Jurisprudence</u>

1. Polluter pays principle

It only makes the polluter responsible for the damage done to the environment. The polluter must not only compensate the victims of the pollution, but also compensate for the restoration of the environmental destruction already caused. This principle has been widely applied by the courts, for which the National Environmental Policy, 2006 had previously indicated the need to move away from the criminal sanction mechanism and introduce a strict civil liability mechanism based on the polluter pays principle.Times have changed and the inadequacy of the applicable criteria of the laws and their application has been sufficiently demonstrated.

The Supreme Court operationalized this principle by dividing the question into five questions.These are who the polluter is, how and when the application of the principle is activated, how to assess damage and determine compensation, what the polluter pays and finally what are the limits of the principle. However, the courts have acted inconsistently in implementing this principle.

2. Public trust doctrine

First application in Indian environmental law in the case of M.C. Mehta vs Kamal Nath and Ors[14], promotes the idea that natural resources do not belong to one person and that it is up to the government and regulators to act as trustees and hold the resources for the free and unhindered use of those resources by others at large Publicity. Once applied, however, it seems quite difficult to see how the doctrine could provide predictability for public trust decision-making. The doctrine needs to become more relevant and find ways to better protect the natural resources it holds in trust.

3. Precautionary principle

This principle, as the name suggests, promotes the implementation of preventive measures in situations that, despite the lack of scientific certainty, could lead to a serious threat or irreversible damage. However, the application of the principle in the Vellore judgment is at odds with the Supreme Court's definition of the principle. There is a lack of clarity in the Court's commitment to this principle and a blurring of the boundaries between two distinct legal principles: precautionary and prevention. This can be helpful in arriving at green court outcomes, but does not bode well for the development of clear case law.

4. Sustainable development

This concept aims to meet people's current needs without compromising future generations' access to similar resources. To elaborate on the Indian Supreme Court's definition of the principle, reference may be made to the judgment in Vellore Citizens' Welfare Forum v. However, Union of India[15], after a critical examination of the Narmada judgment (1999), shows how the Supreme Court "instructionally exploited the inherent vagueness of the principle".

Environment protection beneath the common law

• Negligence

Action beneath negligence may be introduced with the aid of using organising an immediate nexus/connection among the negligence and the harm caused. It additionally calls for the respondent to show that fairly enough care became taken to keep away from such public nuisance as required with the aid of using the law. It is higher defined withinside the case of Naresh Dutt Tyagi v. State of Uttar Pradesh[16], which became a uncomplicated case of negligence. Herein the fumes launched from the leaked insecticides to the close by place via ventilators resulted in the dying of 3 youngsters and a foetus in a pregnant woman.

• Nuisance

This pertains to unlawful interference of one's amusement of land and any legal rightarisingfrom it which might be classified under personal or a common nuisance relying upon the affected individuals. But public nuisance is completely controlled under Section 91 of the Criminal Procedure Code, 1973 (CrPC). It states filing of a suit to demand relief or interim injunction that's possible to cause a public nuisance. CrPC conjointly empowers a judge under Section 133 to require applicable action by restraining a person effecting an act of public nuisance. Within the case of Ramlal v. Mustafabad Oil and Oil Ginning plant [17], the geographical region and Haryana Court discovered that noise arising from a legal activity that's on top of the mandatory threshold is not any defence from attracting the liability of common nuisance. The Indian Penal Code, 1860 conjointly deals with public nuisance which is able to be mentioned later.Section 133 of CrPC, 1973 generally provides for the clean-up of pollution by authorizing a district judge and subdivisional judge to clean up the nuisance. Any order made pursuant to this provision will not be challenged in civil court. The word harassment accustomed in Govind Singh v. In Shanti Swarup[18], the court gave a very liberal interpretation, including in its meaning the removal of substances, the construction of structures, the pursuit of trade and commerce, and the confinement or elimination of all dangerous animals. However, a personal dispute can't depend on this segment and have to be a case of coming near threat affecting the general public interest.

- Strict Liability and Absolute Liability

This principle was established by the case of Rylands v. Fletcher[19] in which a person brings onto his land for his own purposes and collects and stores there anything that can do harm. at his own risk, and if he escapes and causes damage, he is prima facie liable for all damage which is the natural result of his escape. This principle was also recognized in the Indian legal framework in M C Mehta v. Union of India[20] which recognizes strict liability and extends it to absolute liability given the seriousness of the damage caused. Exceptions to strict liability include acts of God, fault of the plaintiff, an act of a third party, any act committed after obtaining the plaintiff's express or implied consent, or where the defendant uses the land naturally.The concept of absolute liability also developed from the above-mentioned MC Mehta case, which was based on the strict liability rule and stipulated that the liability for the damage caused remains with the defendant, regardless of the exceptions to the strict liability rule. This rule states that a person who engages in an inherently dangerous activity and, by engaging in such an activity, causes himself or herself injury as a result of an accident, is fully liable.

Course of Action and Steps Ahead

Although the entire article so far has spoken of the need to criminalize environmental crimes, it needs a separate heading for a better understanding. The current state of affairs reflects very well the inadequacy of the existing institutional framework for sanctions, which has not proven to be as strong a deterrent. Academics have also argued that administrative penalties would be inappropriate when the environmental impact is large, and that is where the penal provisions come in. While there are several problems with the existing laws, some of which are: Fewer regulatory/ enforcement staff required in regulators versus the increasing number of industries, lack of adequate technical knowledge/skills needed to enforce regulations, resistance to change/compromise issues, prevailing attitudes, lack of financial resources in general, with only specific ones species is given importance pollution, lack of an independent regulatory mechanism for environmental policy, etc., an integrated approach would introduce holistic legislation as well as a criminal law approach which would solve most problems automatically.

Criminalizing environmental crimes would also allow the court to question the moral guilt of the accused. Otherwise, we are simply undermining the indirect effects of capitalist costs at the cost of harming an entire community of civilians. Until now, Indian courts and green courts rely on a few prominent principles to impose penalties and liability; However, there is no specific law determining the amount of the penalty. Indian authorities also do not maintain reliable sources for data on sanctions imposed by the courts. Compared to the US, his fines totalled just $74,715 compared to $253,437 for antitrust offenses and $141,351 for other crimes. These righteous ways indicate that although large organizations have to pay for environmental violations, they simply treat them as a cost of doing business. It doesn't necessarily prevent them from doing even more harm to citizens, showing that these monetary and administrative sanctions are not enough.

Criminalizing certain environmental crimes would serve the purpose efficiently. This statement is based on data from the USA, which has done pioneering work in this field. They began criminalizing environmental crimes in the 1980s, and the results have been "concrete," according to one scholar. The US Department of Justice also stated that the Department has filed environmental criminal charges against 911 companies and individuals and that 686 guilty pleas and convictions have been filed. A total of $212,408,903 in criminal penalties was imposed. More than 388 years of imprisonment were imposed, of which almost 191 years correspond to effective imprisonment. A penal code would at least instil fear in people to take environmental laws and prohibitions seriously. One way to move in that direction would be to issue such penalties based on actual damage inflicted rather than the number of sections injured. Depending on the severity, they can impose simple fines or penalties, or severe penalties and criminal sanctions. It may have its own difficulties, such as B. Determining the phase that attracts criminal acts, but that can be better managed by the wisdom of lawmakers.

However, three main models can be invoked that would pave the way for determining such violations. These are the abstract hazard model, the concrete hazard model, and the severe environmental contamination model. In all of these models, two main questions are addressed, whether the criminalization is being carried out because of the violation of the law or whether it should be done because the violation of the law has a strong impact on the general public. Criminal liability could arise solely from violating a rule and not just by causing significant damage. This is based on the "minimum guilt" model by Michael M.O'Hear.

What is really important to consider, however, is the idea that the rule should be enacted in a way that directly/indirectly creates deterrent value. It would also be beneficial to have clear guidelines for sentencing the crime. The organization could have some sort of self-monitoring mechanism to uncover the impact of their violations and reduce sanctions. Another thing to consider is that hefty fines and penalties would also cause the organization to resort to expensive remedies to prevent such violations, which in turn would automatically increase their cost of doing business and therefore the cost of the product to consumers, which is not the Fall seems like a wise way out.

Conclusion

It has been found that there is too much legislation trying to address environmental issues. However, this has only led to more ambiguity and difficulties in implementation. What we need is a strong integrated system that provides a unified holistic approach and effective outcomes. With all principles in place, judicial enforcement mechanisms have had mixed success. In addition to complex external factors, certain institutionalized internal weaknesses of the affect the implementation process, such as the inconsistency of the courts in the implementation of the implementation mechanisms and that their orders require stronger legal justification and better integration into the existing regulatory framework.All of these issues can be efficiently addressed by introducing criminal liability, which would not only save the court time but also add deterrent value. It's time the country exposed the serious criminal consequences that people would face for breaking laws when it comes to environmental destruction.

We as humans have done enough to break the planet, and this planet has given the humans everything issue they need, however owing to the human greed, that's present within the society, has junction rectifier to the present damage. There are that} we tend to humans will recover but it'll take time, but first we need correct law enforcement, to bring a finish to these reasonably activities, and even before that. we want new laws, which are strict enough, to use the principle of deterrence. This paper has catered to bring the crimes against surroundings and life nearer to the crime against humanity, crime against environment and wildlife, ought to be thought of as a criminal offense against humanity. This environment has been there to fulfil every and each would like of the humans, we tend to have to be compelled to watch out of the environment because it has taken our care. The environment doesn't need humans for its existence the humans need environment for his or her survival. In India and round the world we've got several thinkers, many laws, many activists, however it's the role of very single individual that contributes to environment degradation, or surroundings development. we've got several things to do, however we tend to cannot do, until the time we don't seem to be able to save our environment. Finally, we can say, that with each step that we conceive to take towards the environment we should always take solely once assessing every factor, we should follow the principles, and laws. we should always respect and watch out of the environment, as we will only develop till the time life exist during this planet, and existence of life is extremely getting ready to an environment. while not environment there's no life, and while not life there aren't any humans.

CHAPTER SEVEN

THE JUDICIAL INTERPRETATION OF SEAT VS PLACE/ VENUE OF ARBITRATION

Author: Ritwik Prakash, V year of B.Com.,LL.B.(Hons.) from Amity Law School, Noida

Black's Law Dictionary defines "Arbitration" as "An arrangement for taking and abiding by the judgment of selected persons in some disputed matter, instead of carrying to established tribunals of justice, and is intended to avoid the formalities, the delay, the expense and vexation of ordinary litigation". Arbitration is typically characterised as a process of alternative conflict settlement in which the disputing parties pick a neutral arbitrator whose decision is binding on the parties. It is thought to be an out-of-court settlement technique that is more effective, faster, private, and takes less time.

Legal history has spanned millennia, with significant developments in response to changing periods and social, economic, cultural, and political circumstances. Capitalism and liberalism both benefited from industrialization in the 18th century. As a result of these changes, the idea and concept of globalisation emerged, which some authors believe has existed since the beginning of trade and interchange of goods centuries ago.

It is no secret that individuals have disagreements, and traditionally, disagreements have been settled through the old-school approach of litigation. As a result of the increasing complications of globalisation, liberalisation, and the fast speed of life, there has been a massive increase in litigation across all countries. As expected, this has resulted in an overburdening of the courts in practically all nations, prompting many people to consider and develop various sorts of alternative dispute resolution processes (ADR's).Arbitration is one of those techniques which are internationally accepted as a successful method of resolving disagreements peacefully and reaching amicable, mutually beneficial, and agreeable solutions to issues of different complexity. However, the concept of arbitration may be traced back to Greek and Roman city states in the 6th century BC. According to historical documents, Greek city governments used arbitration to settle disputes over land ownership and damages.[i]

In India, the Indian Arbitration Act of 1899 was the first to deal with arbitration, but it only applied to the presidential towns of Calcutta, Bombay, and Madras. Arbitration is also mentioned and referred to in three additional legislative acts: the Indian Contract Act of 1872 (Sections 10 & 28), the Specific Relief Act of 1877 (Section 21), and the Second Schedule of the Civil Procedure Code of 1908. The Arbitration Act, modelled after the English Arbitration Act of 1934, was passed in 1940. However, two different laws regulated the enforcement of a foreign award. The Arbitration (Protocol and Convention) Act of 1937 (for Geneva Convention Awards) and the Foreign Awards (Recognition and Enforcement) Act of 1961 was both enacted (for New York Convention Awards). These acts, however, were fraught with complexity and thus inefficient. Following the 1990s economic liberalization, the Arbitration & Conciliation Act, 1996 was enacted, based on the UNCITRAL Model Law on International Commercial Arbitration, 1985, and the UNCITRAL Conciliation Rules, 1980. So far, it has been updated in 2015 and 2019.

In the context of globalisation, transnational disputes involving entities from other countries have become more widespread, attracting the scrutiny and jurisdiction of their respective countries. International commercial arbitration involving numerous parties from several jurisdictions has raised a number of critical issues. In the case of Naviera Amazonica Peruana SA v. Compania International de Seguros del Peru, the Court of Appeal of England elaborated on the questions to be considered when entering into an arbitration agreement, such as the law applicable to the substantive contract (LexContractus), the law applicable to the arbitration agreement & its performance (LexArbitri), and the law governing the procedure & conduct of arbitration (Curial Law).

The issue of "seat" vs. "venue/place" of arbitration governing the dispute is a critical distinction that arises in international commercial arbitration disputes. While venue/place of arbitration solely refers to the geographical region in which the arbitration proceedings are taking place, seat of arbitration refers to the court/tribunal that has jurisdiction over the proceedings. This has various legal consequences, including the arbitral award's legality and enforceability, the extent of contesting the award by either party/parties, procedural guarantees, the effectiveness and efficiency of conflict settlement, court appeal and review of the award, and so on. [ii]

The Arbitration & Conciliation Act of 1996 fails to define the terms "seat" and "venue" of arbitration, instead using the term "place" under Section 2. (2). India is represented by its location under the act. Furthermore, Section 20, which explains how to determine the location of arbitration, is confusing in its distinction between "seat" and "venue." Despite the Law Commission's 246th report suggesting a slew of amendments to the Act, only a few were implemented through the 2015 revision. Thus, in order to shed some light on this ambiguity, the judiciary has taken it upon itself time and again to provide clarity on these phrases.

The seat may be distinct, distinct, and independent of the venue or site of arbitration. The term "seat" refers to the tribunal or court that has jurisdiction over the arbitral proceedings, whereas "venue" solely refers to the country or region/area where the proceedings are being held. As a result, the seat is more important than the venue because it is the courts of that location that will have supervisory jurisdiction over the essential subjects before it.

Since the act itself is ambiguous on certain terms, the judiciary has stepped in to provide explanation on such clauses of the act. After its enactment, one of the earliest cases that later went on to be reversed was Bhatia International v. Bulk Trading SA. In this case the apex court elaborated upon the interpretation of Section 2 (2) of the Arbitration & Conciliation Act, 1996. It was held that an international commercial arbitration involving an Indian party would confer jurisdiction on Indian Courts.

In the case of Bharat Aluminium Co. v. Kaiser Aluminium Technical Services Inc.(BALCO), the court reversed its judgement in the 2002 case of Bhatia International v. Bulk Trading SA. The Supreme Court ruled that Part I of the Act only applies if the seat of arbitration is in India, and that Section 2 (2), when combined with Section 20, suggests that the Act lacks extraterritoriality. It was also determined that under the Act, there is a distinction between the terms "seat" and "venue." While Sections 20 (1) and (2) [which elaborate on the parties' right to select the place of arbitration, and in the absence of such selection authorises the tribunal to determine the same] use the term place, which is equivalent to "seat," Section 20 (3) [which allows the tribunal to meet at any location for the sake of convenience] uses the term "venue."[iii]

The recommendation of the Law Commission's 246th Report to replace the words "place" and "venue" with "seat" and "venue" never materialised, and the same was reiterated by the Supreme Court in the case of Enercon (India) Ltd. v. Enercon GmbH (Enercon), in which the court laid down the "closest & most intimate connection test" to determine the "seat" of arbitration. The Delhi High Court found in Antrix Corporation Ltd v Devas Multimedia Pvt Ltd. that the "seat" of arbitration and the court of cause of proceedings have concurrent jurisdiction, however this decision was overturned in the BGS Soma case, which is discussed below.

In the case of Roger Shahshoua v. Mukesh Sharma, to distinguish between "seat" and "venue," the condition of "substantial contrary indicia" was recognised. The ruling in the case of Union of India v. Hardy Exploration & Production was pivotal in bringing some clarity to the situation. In this particular issue, Hardy Exploration and the Government of India agreed to resolve conflicts through arbitration.

The contract's arbitration clause designated "Kuala Lumpur" as the "forum" for arbitration, with the UNCITRAL Model Law of International Commercial Arbitration of 1985 governing the proceedings. The award, which was in favour of Hardy Exploration, was signed by both parties but contested by the Government of India in the Delhi High Court under Section 34 of the Arbitration & Conciliation Act, 1996, with the court ruling that it, was not within its jurisdiction to consider the matter. The case further went to the apex court with the issue being whether "seat" & "venue" specified the same thing if venue is, but seat is not specifically mentioned in the arbitration agreement.It was determined that the terms "seat" and "venue" meant different things, and that "venue of arbitration" can only be interpreted as "seat of arbitration" if the arbitration agreement expressly states so and other articles of the agreement imply the same. Because the "seat of arbitration" was not in Kuala Lumpur, the verdict might be contested in Indian courts under Section 34. This distinction between "seat" & "venue" of arbitration was liquefied in Brahmani River Pellets v.

Kamachi Industries, wherein it was held that "seat" & "venue" of arbitration would mean the same thing if it was not expressly mentioned so in the agreement. [iv]

In BGS SGS Soma v. NHPC, some clarity regarding the stand of the apex court on this confusion was reached as the judgement referred back to the reasoning given in the previous cases of BALCO & Roger Shahshoua. Despite being hailed as a significant judgement, the case has not done particularly much in bringing about a resolution to the debate. More recently, the case of MankastuImpex Private Limited vs. Air visual Limited, the Supreme Court unfortunately, it contributes to the general lack of clarity on the matter.The Court noted that the seat defined the applicable law guiding the arbitration procedures as well as the scope of judicial review of the arbitration result.

To sum up, In a country where the court has taken an active part in casting light on confusing terminology, phrases, articles, and clauses, one finds that it has failed to do so in the instance of Sections 2 (2) and 20 (1), (2), and (3) of the Arbitration and Conciliation Act, 1996. Riddled with ambiguities and varying interpretations, it creates a highly hazy image in front of parties that may seek to use arbitration as an alternate conflict resolution tool to traditional litigation.

In order to make it easier for parties, the court must take a firm stand once & for all to resolve the hazy cloud hanging around these sections of the Act. The court in the case MankastuImpex Private Limited vs. Air visual Limited clearly stated that the mere language "place of arbitration" could not be used to determine the seat, and that court should consider other terms in the agreement as well as the behaviour of the parties to determine the seat of arbitration. Although the court is trying its best, it has to look into all the different aspects that may be impacted whilst doing so & thus I believe it is taking such a long time to reach a conclusive solution to the debate around the terms "seat" &"venue" of arbitration

CHAPTER EIGHT

IMPACT OF ARTIFICIAL INTELLIGENCE ON INTELLECTUAL PROPERTY RIGHTS

Author: Visheshta Kalra, V year of BBA.,LL.B.(H) from Amity Law School, Noida

Co-author: Ritwik Prakash, V year of B.Com.,LL.B.(H) from Amity Law School, Noida

ABSTARCT

Artificial intelligence, which once seemed like a distant dream, has now crossed over from science fiction movies into our reality and in the last few years has gained momentum and made great strides in almost every field. No part of artificial intelligence remains untouched, and intellectual property rights are no exception. The influence of artificial intelligence on intellectual property rights, on the one hand, a novelist has the right to record existing inventions, as well as his ideas and more. Provide a mechanism, but on the other hand artificial intelligence may be a threat to novelty and creativity. Intellectual heart and soul.This paper will examine in detail the impact of artificial intelligence on intellectual property rights, the advantages and disadvantages of artificial intelligence on creativity and innovation. It also examines the future field of artificial intelligence in intellectual property rights.

Keywords: Artificial Intelligence, Intellectual Property Rights, Copyright Law, Patent Law

INTRODUCTION

In recent years we have witnessed an unbridled growthof artificial intelligence (referred to as AI in this document), and it is something capable of performing simple tasks such as calculations perform really simple tasks complex. Put simply, AI will be able to do everything a human can do and even more in the near future. There is still a lot of ambiguity surrounding AI, and the pros and cons of AI is one of the most debated topics these days. Although there is no universally accepted definition of AI, the most basic understanding is that it is about the development of machines and software that can perform functions that generally require human intelligence.

No There is no doubt that the field of intellectual property is not affected by AI and that the intersection of AI and intellectual property could be two facets. On the one hand, it can be an advantage in the field of intellectual property, but it can also pose a threat.

This document discusses in detail the impact of AI on intellectual property with particular reference to copyright, patents and traditional knowledge, and also discusses in detail liability in the event of infringement of intellectual property rights.

FUTURE OF ARTIFICIAL INTELLIGENCE

At present, the AI has been able to perform the tasks related to human intelligenceand the research and development on the AI is still ongoing and the functions that the AI will in near Future can run Future The future is beyond imagination. But if we talk about the advantages, we must not forget that in the end it is about a machine and for a machine, and there were cases when the machine was removed from the programmer's control, and began to perform tasks on its own. Well, these tasks can be constructive or destructive, but it becomes difficult to control the AI machine or program when it starts to perform actions on its own and goes beyond the programmer's hands. Although A lot has happened in the field of artificial intelligence, but there are still many ambiguities that still prevail and there is hope that in the near future this will be resolved in and we will have a clear roadmap on how far AI in the People can act in life andalso in inventions.

ARTIFICIAL INTELLIGENCE AND COPYRIGHT

In general, copyright is a right granted to someone who has created their original work, and the work can be a literary work, song, any softwareetc.

Although the intersection of AI and copyright is not new and has been going on for many years, there was previously no dispute as to who will own the copyright of the work because the program or machine only functioned as a tool to create this work like pencil and paper and the idea or the work belonged to the programmer but with the advancement in AI and as we create machines with human intelligence capable of creating an original work by themselves , then the question is who will have the copyright, it asks whether the copyright goes to the programmer or to the AI machine or the program. Machine learning is something within the purview of AI that involves feeding data into the machine or program and enabling the machine AI to create original work done by Humans are independent.

Therefore, the growth of AI has also led to many ambiguities regarding copyright and there is a need for clear rules and guidelines, otherwise there is a high likelihood of dispute.

<u>ARTIFICIAL INTELLIGENCE AND PATENT</u>

The interface between artificial intelligence and patent law is currently picking up speed. Although on the one hand AI will prove to be an asset to patent protection, patent research, patent search tools and also to inventors by giving them an early idea if a similar system exists. idea or not. The patent is about invention and innovation, and AI capable of human intelligence can make inventions without human input or intervention. When it comes to patents and AI, we need to look specifically at certain areas like:

Weapons: there is a global movement in warfare using AI machines and programs. While the dispute over how AI is regulated under international humanitarian law is not beyond the scope of this document, the issue that when an AI machine or program makes a weapon, there is ambiguity as to who is doing it becomes. received the patent for it.

Medicine/Pharmaceutical: When it comes to patents, the pharmaceutical industry or inventions, drugs are the top priority. Now, if there is a situation where the AI successfully produces a drug, a patent problem arises. For example, in the current situation where the whole world is looking for a vaccine against the global pandemic coronavirus and if in such a situation an AI machine invents a vaccine for it, there will be a lot of ambiguity about who will have the patent. of the vaccine, whether it goes to the machine or the AI program, or to the programmer who created that machine, or to the buyer of the vaccine. Unless this issue is resolved, it cannot be determined how and at what cost the vaccine will be made available to other nations. It is therefore necessary to nip these problems in the bud.

Road Safety:Many programs are developed to ensure road safety, but the number of road deaths cannot be ignored either. There is a possibility that AI can find a solution to this, where we can prevent the loss of human life, in the same way that self-driving cars can be invented. Apart from that, there are companies that are already working on this aspect of road safety and are using AI. Like Microsoft is developing facial recognition software that monitors driver behavior and can generate a timely warning to avoid accidents.

New Technologies: We invent many inventions every day and patent law is about innovation and invention. As discussed above, in the case of an invention of an AI machine or a programmer, a clear picture is needed of who holds the patent, whether the patent belongs to that machine or goes to the programmer.

ARTIFICIAL INTELLIGENCE AND TRADITIONAL KNOWLEDGE

Traditional knowledge is something (perhaps a skill or some know-how or practice) acquired or followed from time to time. Knowledge is passed from one generation to another generation by this community. There may be instances where the AI can violate traditional knowledge by using summaries of traditional knowledge already available.

So, in light of the discussion mentioned above, there could be a possibility that the machine or the program of artificial intelligence could violate traditional knowledge that is part of the rich heritage of many communities.

LIABILITY OF INFRINGEMENT

This is one of the most debated topics as to who is liable when there is violation of Intellectual Property Rights through an AI gadget. Whether the programmer could be accountable or whether or not the gadget could be accountable or whether or not all and sundry else could be accountable. There is still ambiguity concerning this aspect.

If the programmer is aware that the machine tends to infringe intellectual property rights, then in that case the responsibility lies with the programmer since he was aware of the infringement behind the creation of that program or machine. However, in the event that the programmer has no knowledge or intent to infringe the intellectual property rights, and yet the machine or AI program infringes the intellectual property rights, it willbe difficult for to determine who is responsible .

Therefore, this is another aspect that is ambiguous, and there is a gap that needs to be filled in order to determine the responsibility of the machine or the artificial intelligence program. If the offense is such as to give rise to criminal liability, how will the AI be individually criminally liable?

As we noted above, the issue of liability is a matter of concern and should be else it would lead to much argument and confusion.

CONCLUSION

There is no doubt that artificial intelligence can prove to be an advantage in the field of intellectual property rights to a certain extent, since it can make many inventions that can cost and help any human being years. in the progress of nations, but then there are many gaps and ambiguities regarding the use of artificial intelligence in intellectual property rights, but AI can also pose a threat as there are problems in determining responsibility in case of infringement. Guidelines and rules are needed regarding artificial intelligence and how liability is determined. It also needs to be clarified who will own the copyrights, patents or other intellectual property rights to the work or invention of the AI.

Therefore, artificial intelligence is still in a very early stage and shows great growth is expected. and the debate on the impact of artificial intelligence will never end, either in any sector or specifically in relation to intellectual property rights,until rules are established on the use of AI, their responsibilities and the extent AI is allowed to intervene.A roadmap for AI, its operation, control and accountability is urgently needed given the speed at which AI is growing today.

In short, AI is very beneficial when under the programmer's control, but the moment it starts to work independently without external control, it could pose a threat not only to the intellectual property area , but also for everyone in general.

Authors' Biography

Visheshta Kalra

My name is Visheshta Kalra. I'm 22 years old. Born and brought up in Chandigarh. I am a 5th year law student completing my BBA.LLB (H) from Amity Law School, Noida. I like challenges which would enhance my caliber

Ritwik Prakash

My name is Ritwik Prakash. I'm 22 years old. I am a 5th year law student completing my B.COM LLB (H) from Amity Law School, Noida. An optimistic, innovative, observant and motivated person who has got few aspirations alive that keep me moving ahead and teach me to never quit.

CHAPTER NINE

SHOULD WE ALL BE FEMINISTS

Author: Raushni Ranjan Pradhan, IV year of B.A.,LL.B.(Hons.) from Law college Dehradun

INTRODUCTION

The word feminism or feminist was first used in France and Netherlands which means "the qualities of females". The origin of feminism is from Latin word "Famina" which means "The Women". First time the word feminsmused in 1890. The word feminsm was first time coined by Charles forier. The term feminism nowadays refer the political, economic and social equality of all humans and to organize activities on women's behalf. According to English Dictionary the word feminismmeans "the confidence that women should be allowed the same rights, power and fortuity as men and be delicacy in the same way, or the set of activities intended to achieve this state". Feminism can be simply defined as equality. Feminism is nothing a revolt against the unequal treatment to women.

This movement is based on the to remove the disparity between men and women and to establish egalitarian society. Albeit Government gave the status of enfranchisement to the women but chauvinism society still exists. The feminism deals with equal opportunities not with biological differences. We find that womenis treated unidentical in society and they are consider lower to men this thing grown in mind of women and from therethe feminist movement started. Today's feminismis direct productof 1960s Women'sMovement but let thinks about the root of this movement that burgeon in 1960s . The radicle of feminist goes in 1792 MARY WOLLSTONECRAFT and her book called A Vindication Of Rights Of Women's Structures considered as a first book in feminism. In this book she discusses the male writer Milton, Rousseau's and she talks about how they portrait women and what are the perspectives they expressed in their book.

IMPORTANCE OF FEMINISM

Feminism and why remains important, for several years women are bigotry for various reasons they were denied for basic rights and treated as second class citizens. Even today also women is treated unequalon men. Global idea man and women both deserveequal rights within the field of social, political economical etc. The feminist campaign in history marked the importance of women and provided right to vote and right publically property to women. The feminisim isn't just important for women but for every sex, gender, caste, creed and more. A awfully common misconception is that only women are often feminist it's absolutely wrong. It derives for equality for women not superiority of women . In other words it benefits both men and women. For instance why it advocates women must be free and therefore the same time it also advocates why man should be head of family. We must always give freedom to all or any most significantly it's essential for youth to induce people to get indulged in feminism movement . The very famous author Chimamanda Ngozi Adichie has written book "We should all Be Feminists" born in September 1977,is a Nigerian writer of fiction and non – fiction. In " We should All be Feminists "(2012), she shares her opinion on being an African feminist within the twenty first century. She talks about constructive gender that how man and women treated in society at a given point of your time . She shares her thoughts on feminism, sexuality and mix reflections supported on her personal experiences and theoretical observations. The movement we discuss feminism it means rallying for equality ,freedom etc. She contains a somewhat change oriented stance. She views gender construction as a matter of injustice in present day and views anger as capable of bringing about positive change in society. Display faith within the human ability to reinvent themselves. Yes, we should always be Feminists the word feminsm is indeed also connected with a particular movement that has fought very hard to place these items on the social agenda.In essence, it's about men and women beingequal within the sense of contribute in social life,in life as a full. Feminism isn't try and take From man but try and raise same level as a person have. Feminism not only implies that you suspectin quality of success. Feminismis all about equity.

First wave of feminism was held at Seneca falls convention (1848) were both men and women accumulate together and talks about women'srights. Second wave of feminismstarted in 1960sduring this wave they talkedabout racism and that they took decisionthat this time the crownof Miss AmericaPageant will be given to black women. The most focus of this wave was the reproduction rights of women. Feminism impliesthat there shouldbe equal rightsgiven to men and women. The liberalfeminism means freedomand there mustn'tbe any discrimination. Socialist feminismsays that discrimination is happening becauseof capitalism. The most disparitywas men use to inducemore wages than women. The fight of feminism is to provide full gender equality in law and in actual practiceand unfasten all kind of disparity betweenmen and women. Traditionally, male phenomenology have denied the importance of the experiential. Feminist epistemology, on the other hand is grounded in the lives realities of women's lives though this critical perspective often locates feminist as " other" in malestream disciplines. Within the new millennium many women throughout the globe are campaigning, organizing and dealing simultaneously to boost theirlives. The status of feminismtoday is howeverhighly ambivalent. On the one hand it seems to be clearlysuccessful story that has transformed both dominant ideologies and therefore material conditions of women's lives which continues to inspire women throughout the world. In many countries of the world today ,youngwomen see legal, economic, political, social, sexualand reproductive rightsand freedoms as obvious entitlements instead of feministdemands. Feminism can seem at the best an out – dated and at the worst a threat to loving relationships between men and women or an anti-male obstacle to genuine equality.Many other women who appear to be pursuing feminist goals reject the feminist label,which they see as elitista kind of political and cultural imperialism on the a part of white, westernwomen who are privileged in most ways.Feminists are profoundly and at times bitterly divided, not only over political priorities and methods, but also over goals.

The feministconcept of patriarchy a term which has an earlier and very differentusage in conventional political theory was first set out by Kate Millett in sexual politics millett argued that in all known societies the relationship between sexes has been based on men's power over women. Concept of patriarchy is said to be descriptive and a historical rather than analytical. It is unable to explain the genesis of hegemonic or to provide a comprehensible strategy for ending it. We should all be feminist is the end of gender and the creationof new human beings who are self- determining and fully participate in the development of their own constantly evolvingsubjectivity. We couldthink of this position as a feminist humanist position. Women as bearer of Indian culture was a very patriarchal construct. Nationalists for instance were praising child marriage, saying it's a wonderful Indian custom. You can imagine the kind of fraught relationship the kind of tense relationship that would result when women want to continue to petition the British state, saying, we want to raise the age of Marriage. We don't think it's a wonderful Indian custom. Which is what these early social reformers, these women, did. This is why when feminism becomes the name of the women'smovement, feminists are frequently accusedof betraying the nation. In India the thought of feminism was that it was influenced by western cultures, and to be a good Indian woman was to be non- western in terms of what made for this very interesting, peculiar and somewhat unique to India,kind of relationship between feminism, Indianculture and the nation.

<u>CONCLUSION</u>

The feminist claim that women should have the identical rights and freedoms as men has beenlargely relinquish in western society. Issues like abortion, harassment, domestic violence, childcare and parental leave have entered the mainstream of political debate instead of being seen as purely personal concerns. The importance of women's amateur work has become accumulating visible in official economic statistics. So we must look get into cultural and community for creating this dream in actually. We are still on journey so we must continue this mission to achieve success. Feminismhas come along way and women definitely due have more rights. Women are so treated inferior to men in many aspectsin society but we can work and take one step at the time to improvethe conditions. In 2018 it was accepted that it will take another 100 years to achieve global generation equality. But in the year 2019 the number decreasesto 99.5 years. Eventhough the estimated number of years goes down it still isolated .The foremost important steps that ought to be taken regarding feminism is that to teach the next generation about feminism they all should aware about this , and increase femalerepresentation in positionsof power. Let'stake a demeanor and make gender equality a reality.

www.ingramcontent.com/pod-product-compliance
Lightning Source LLC
Chambersburg PA
CBHW052240150726
48002CB00003B/1511